This Coloring Book Belongs To

Color Palette

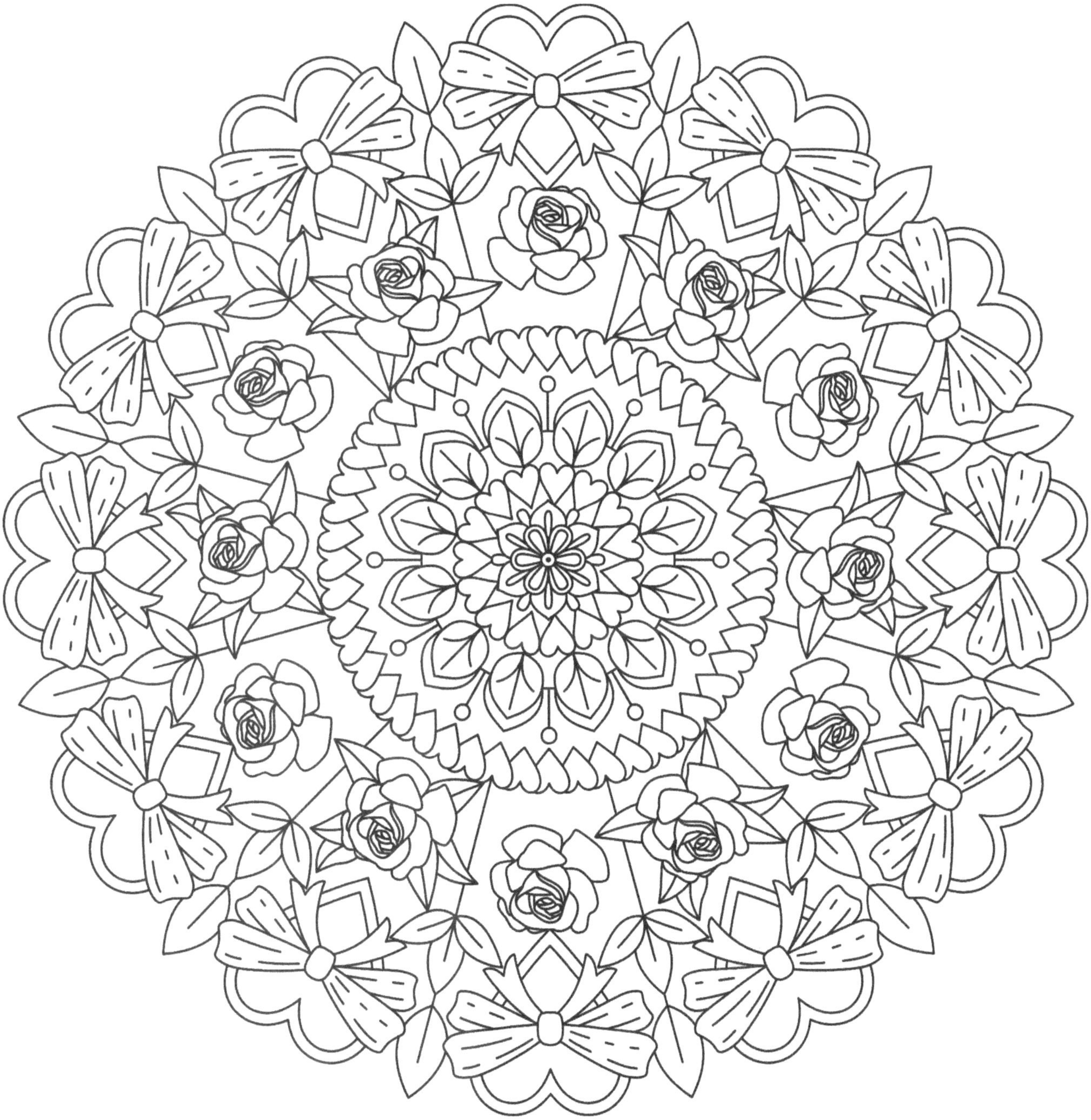

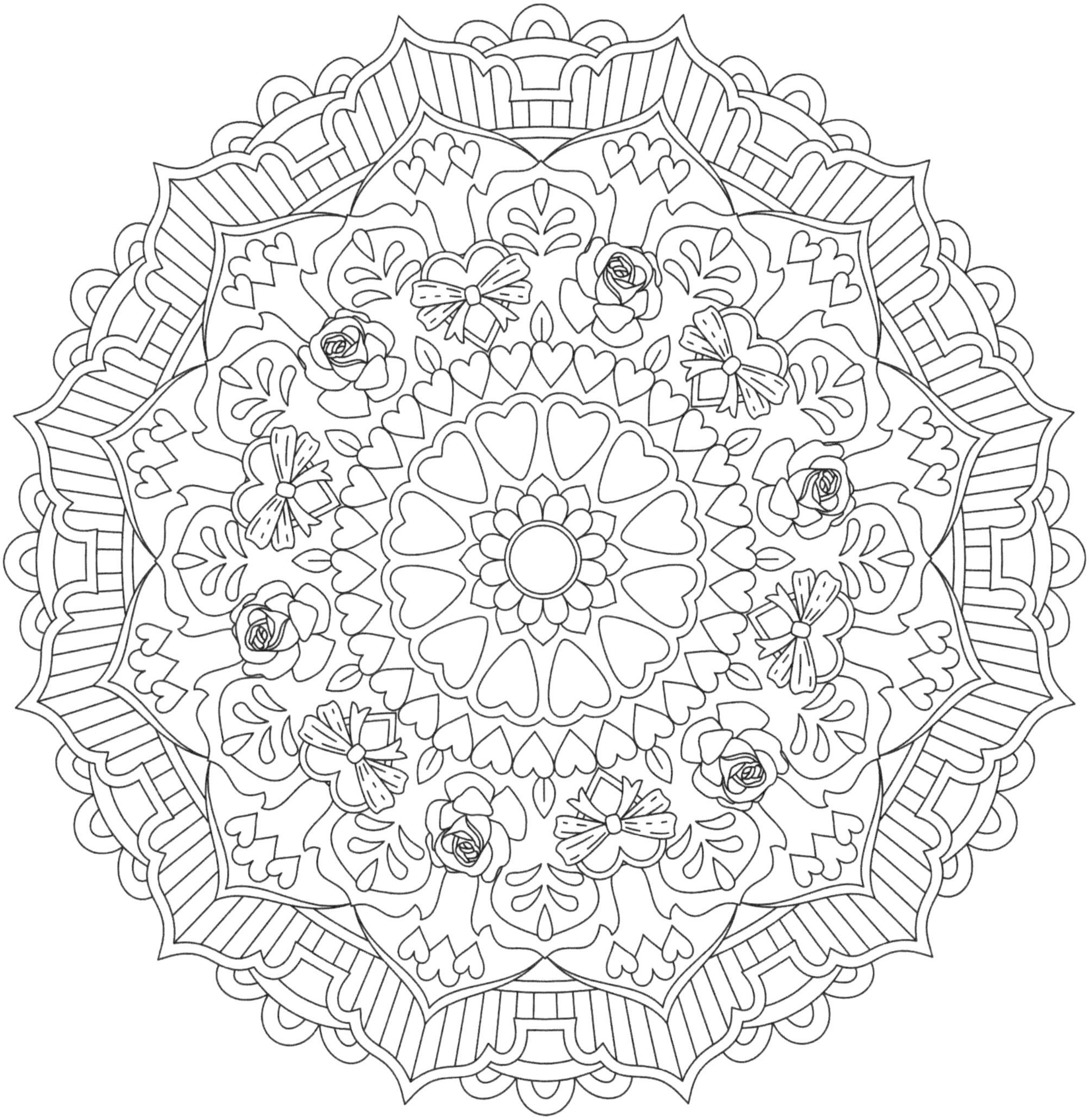

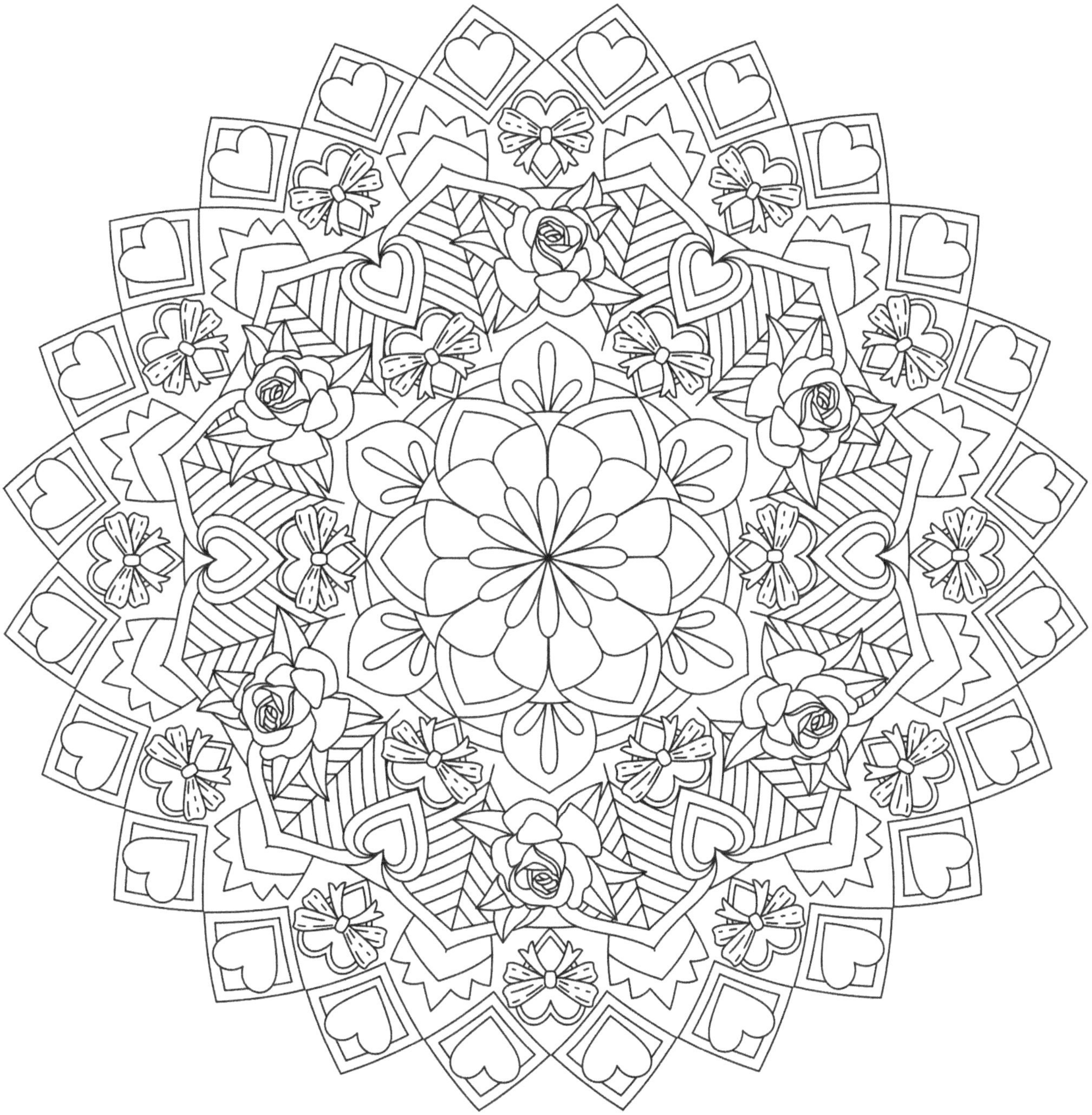

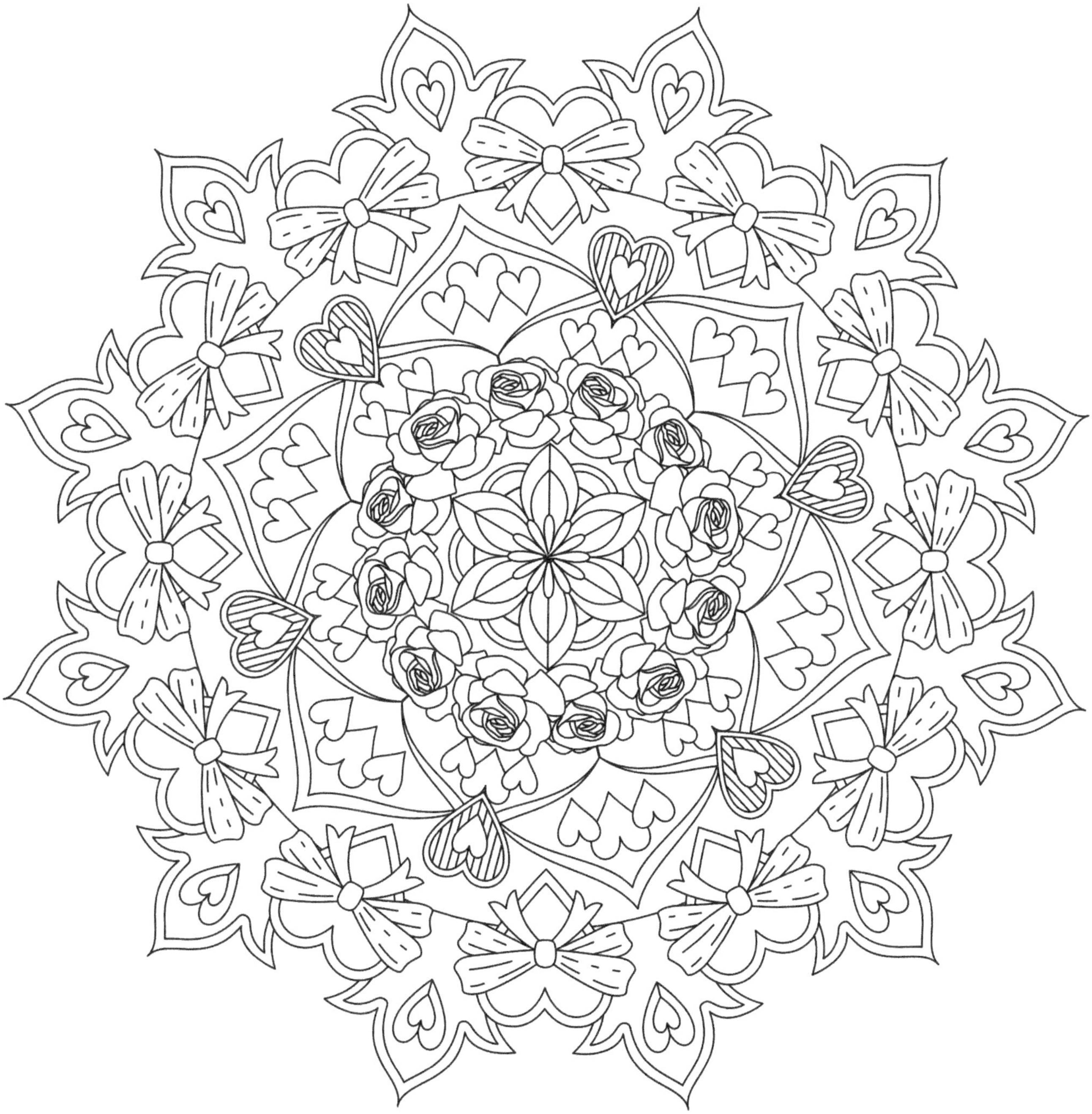

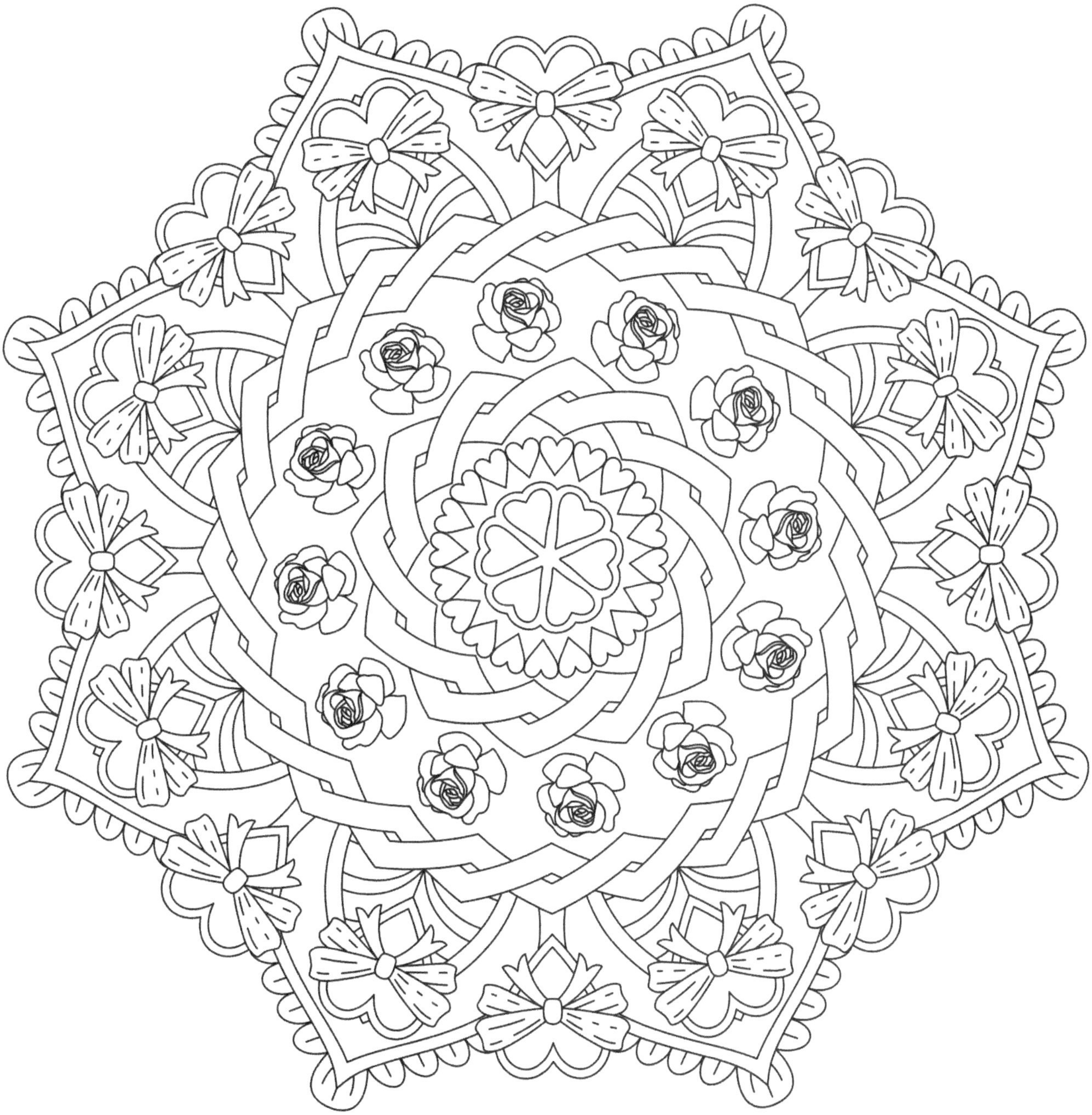

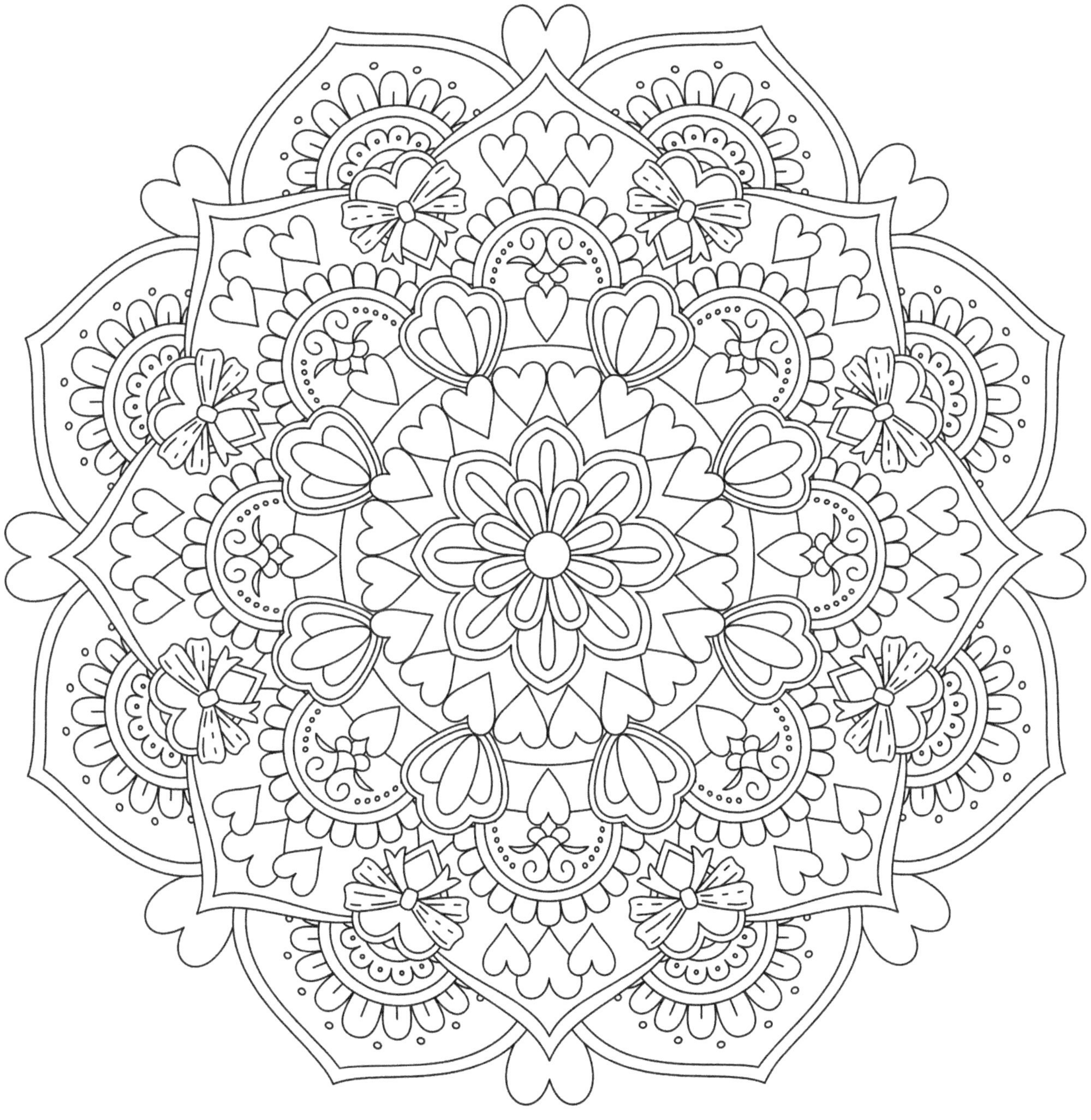

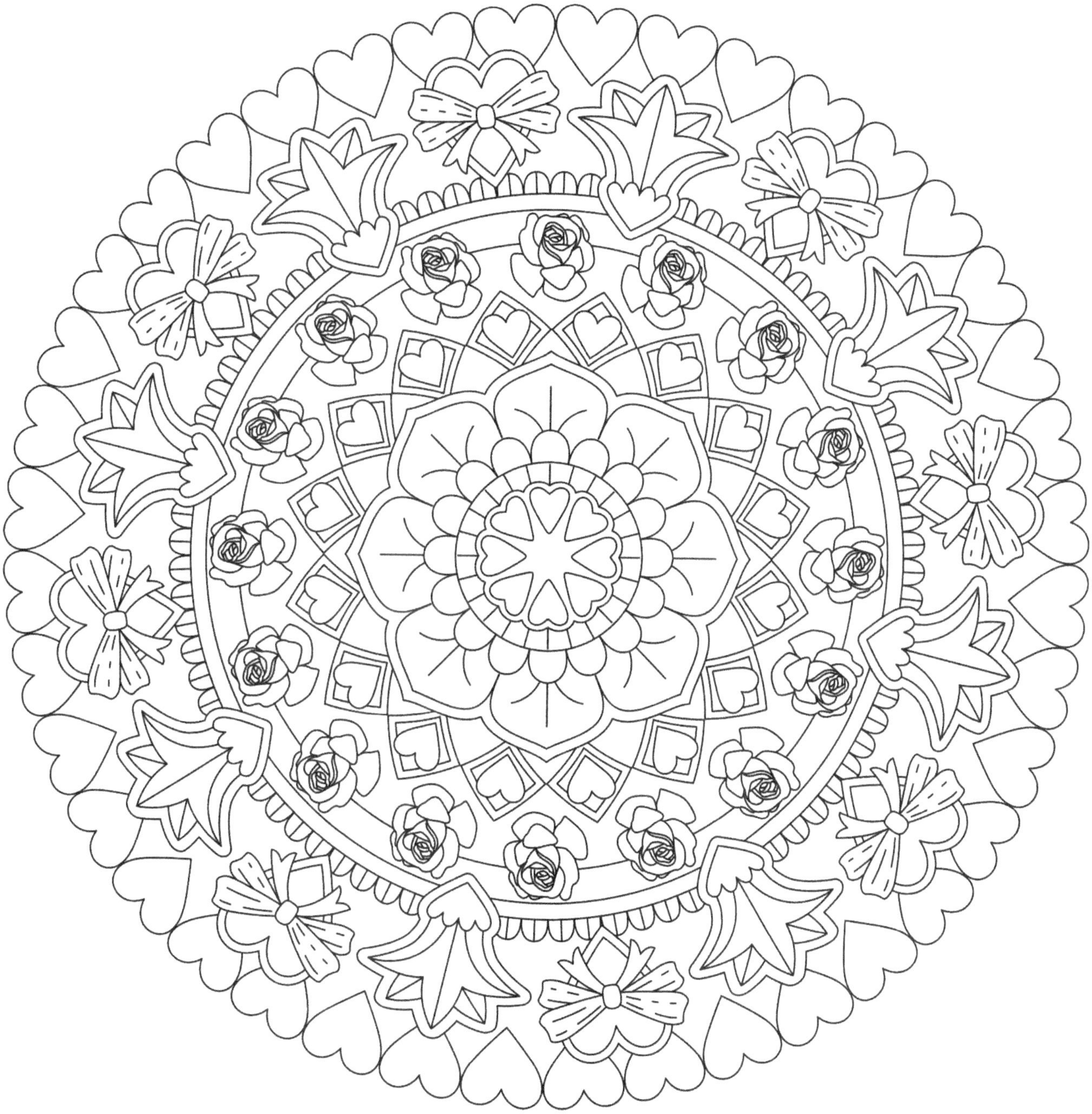

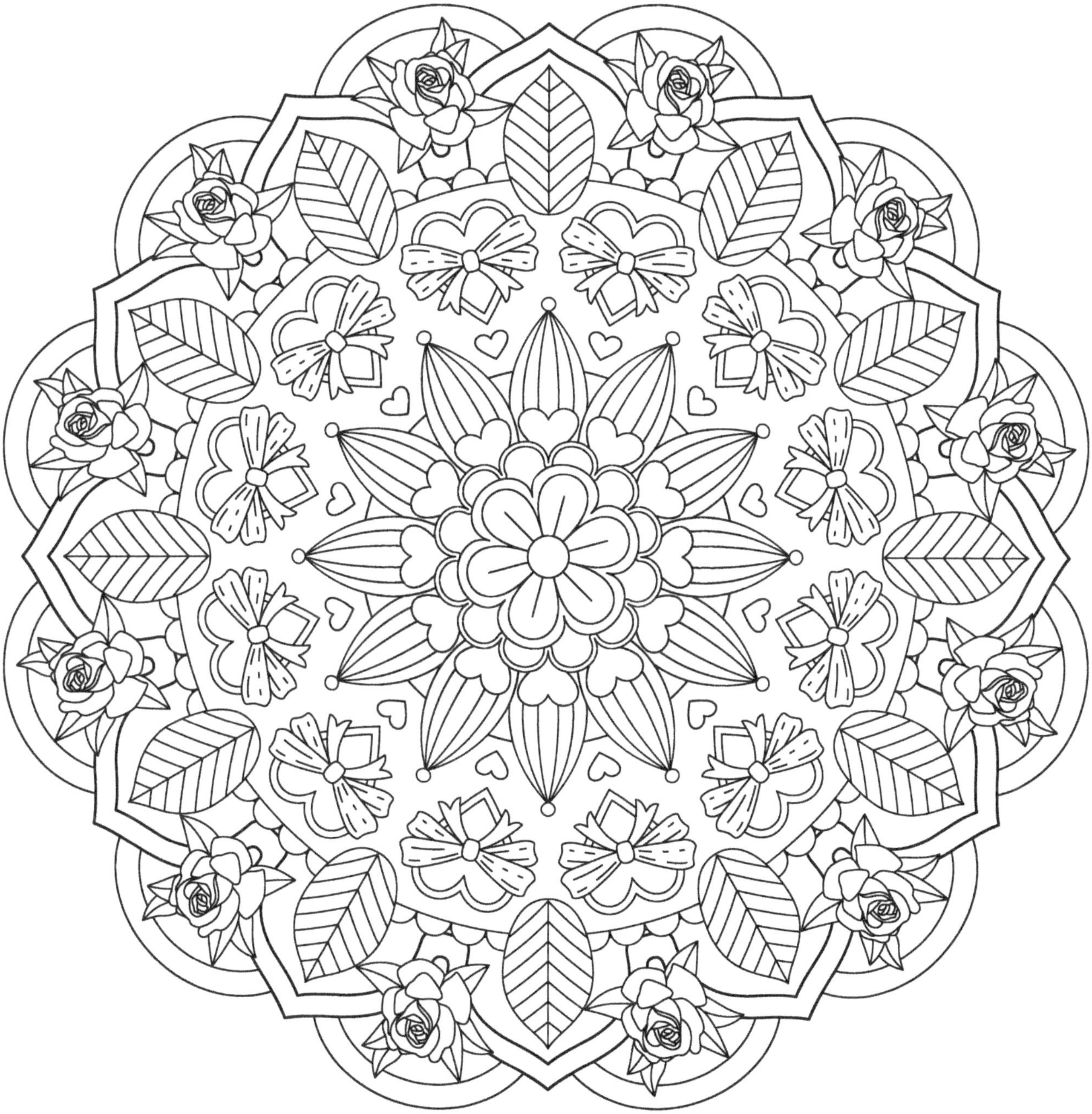

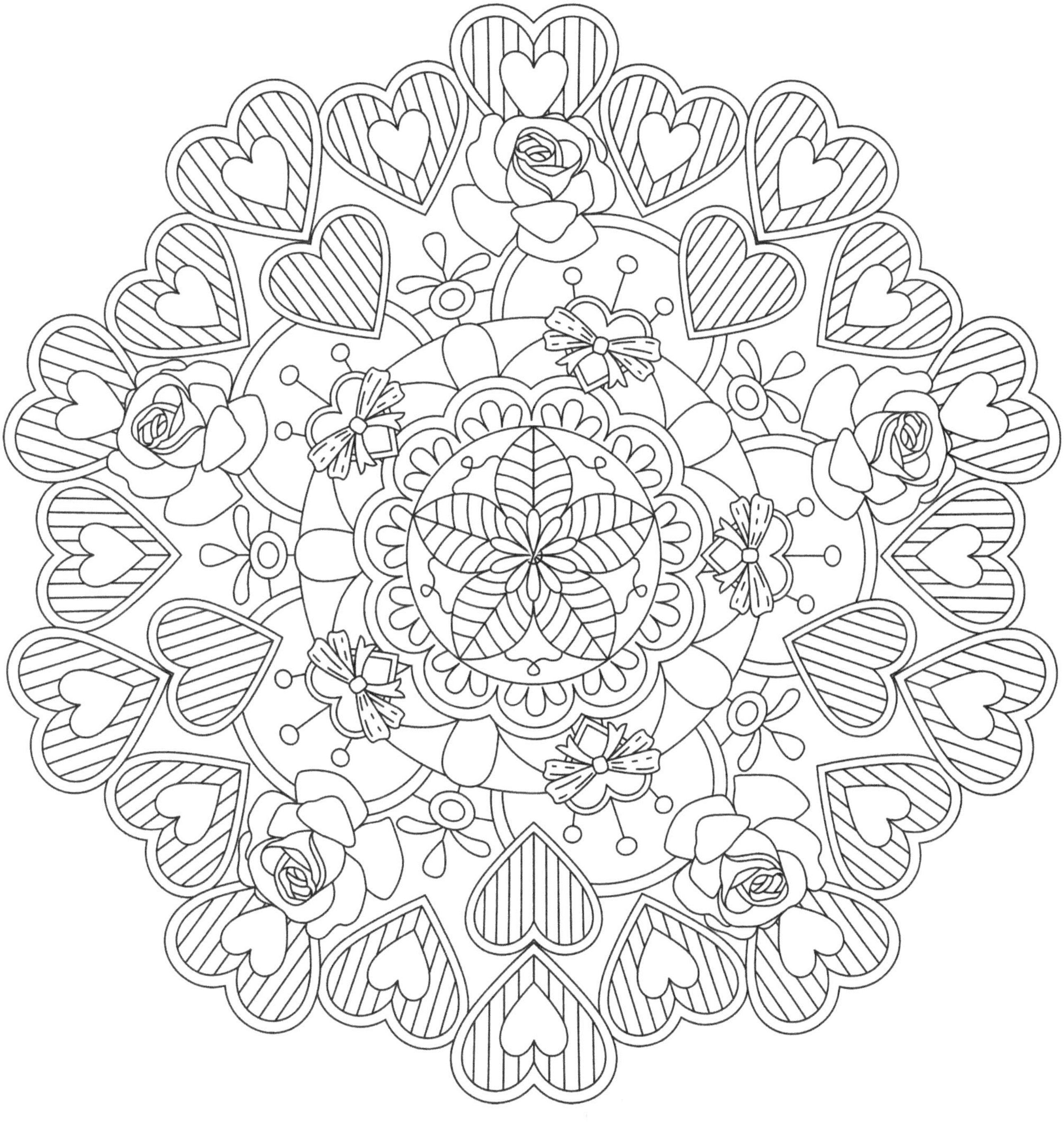

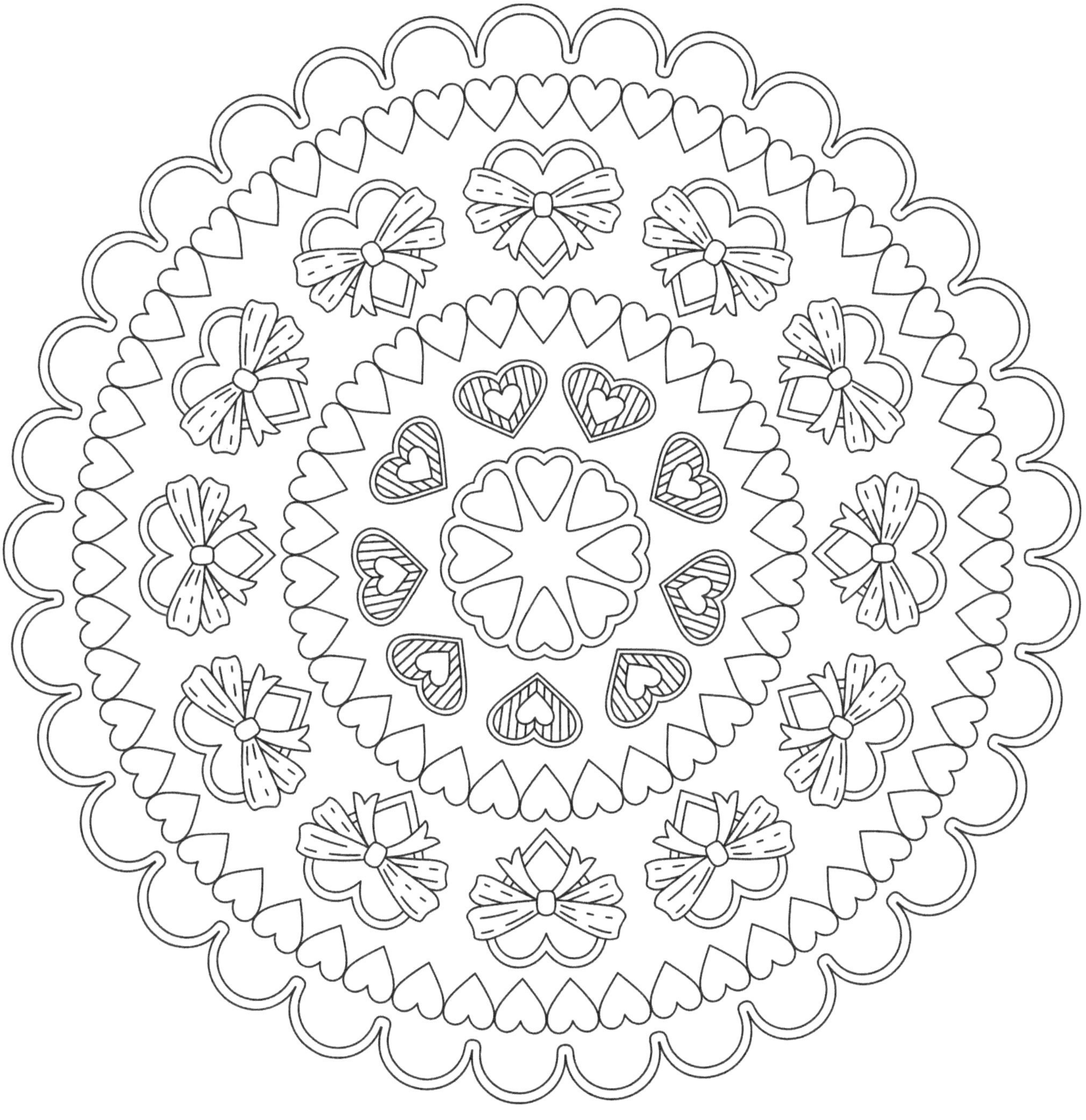

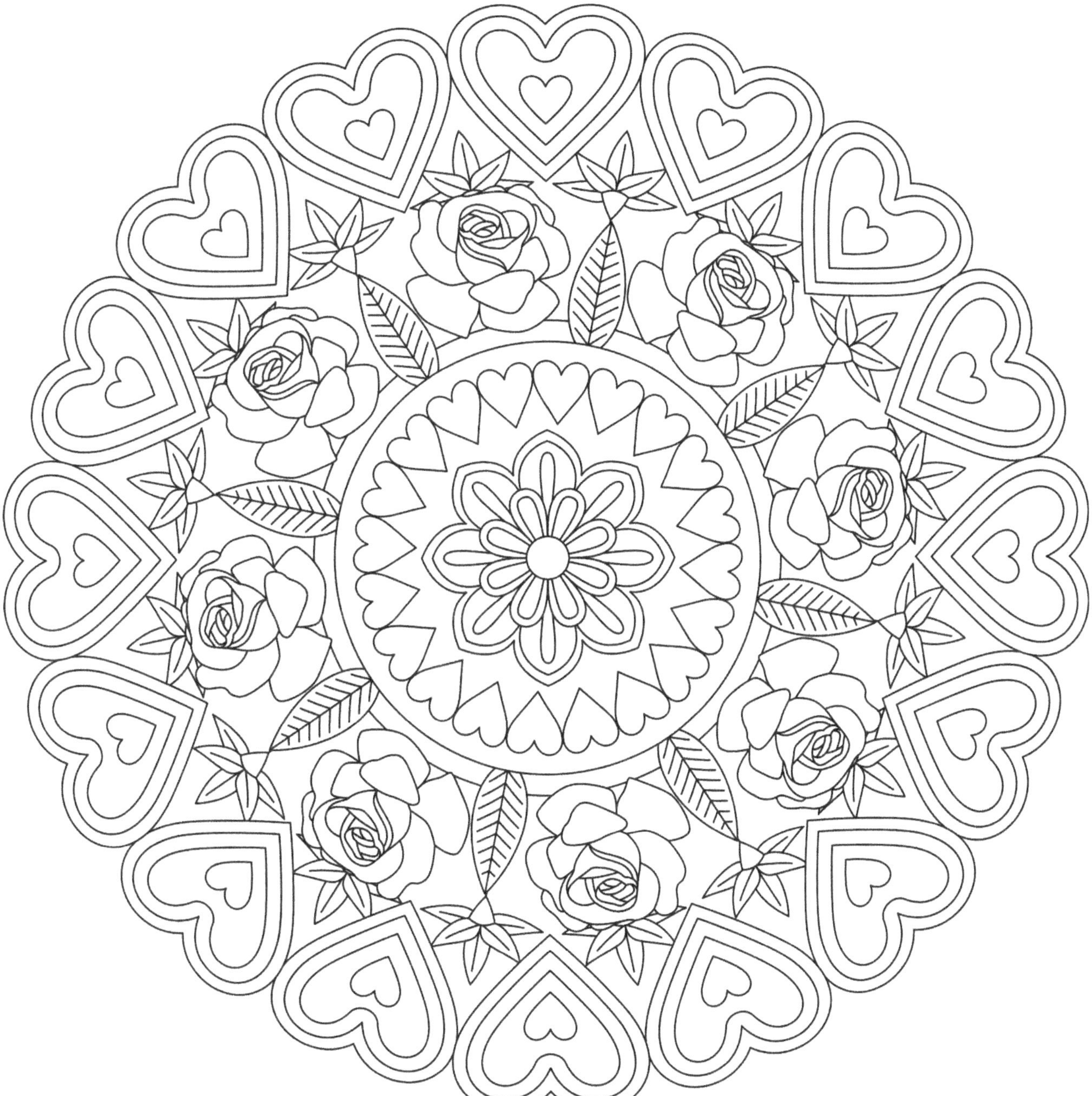

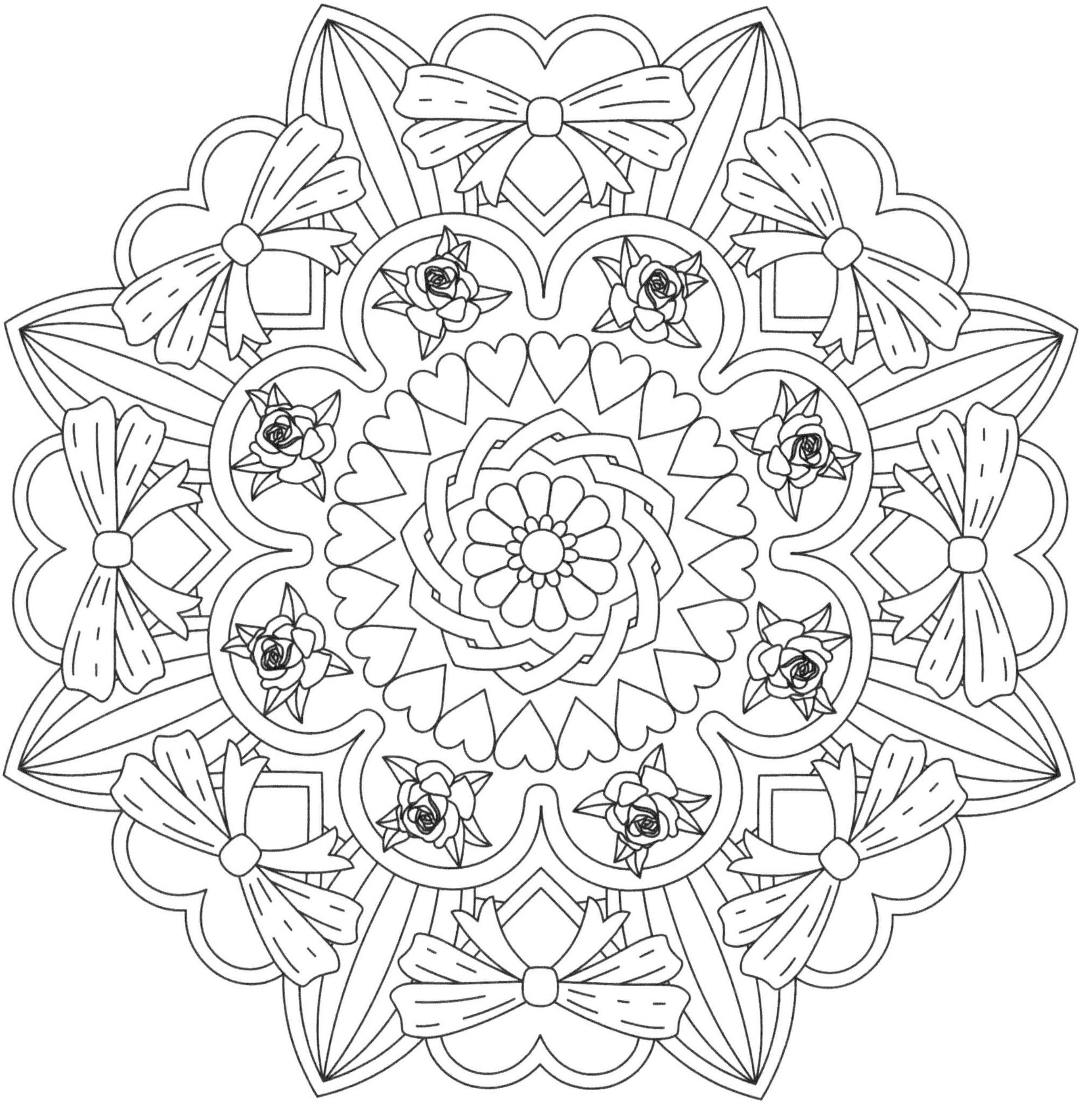

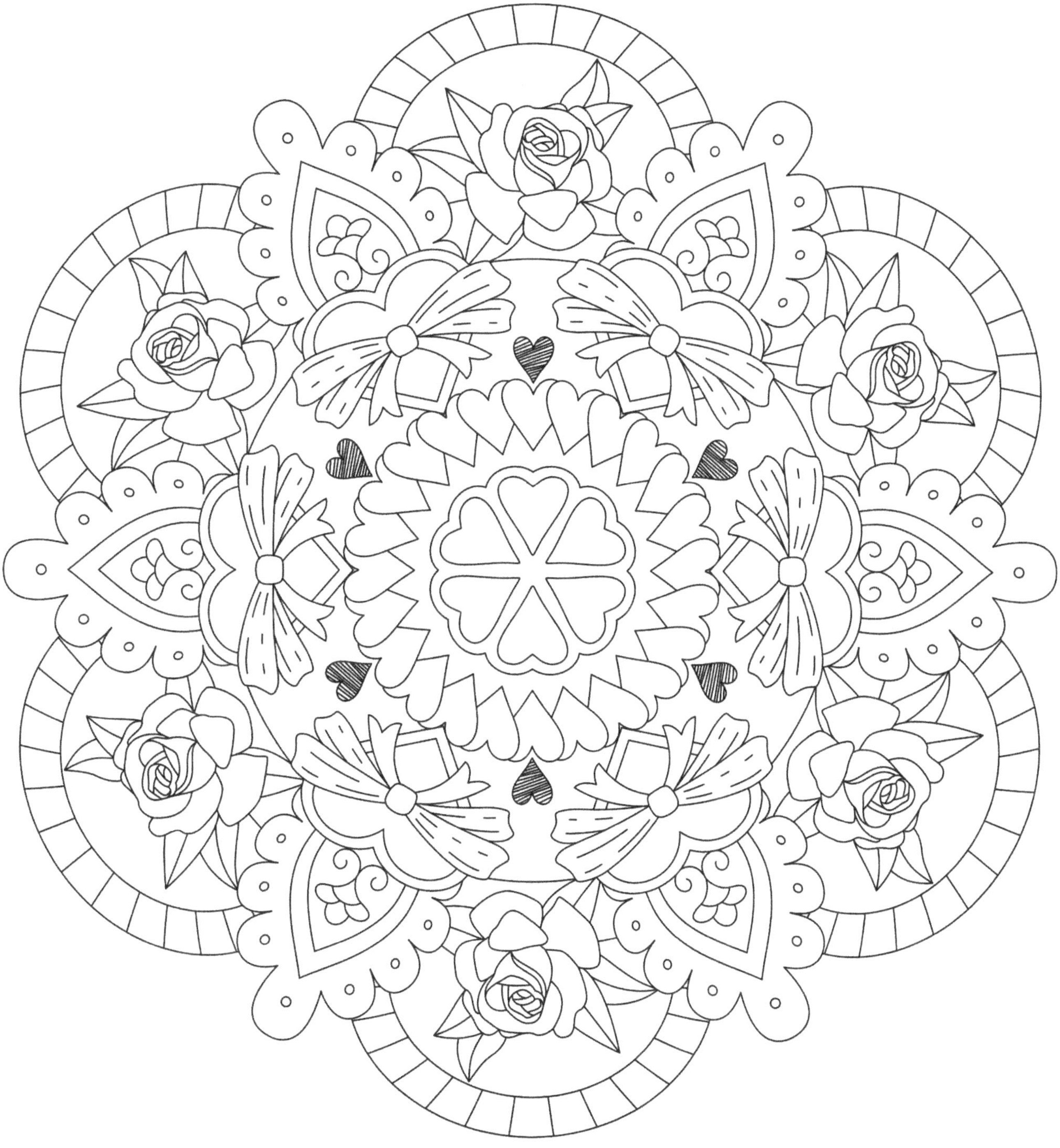

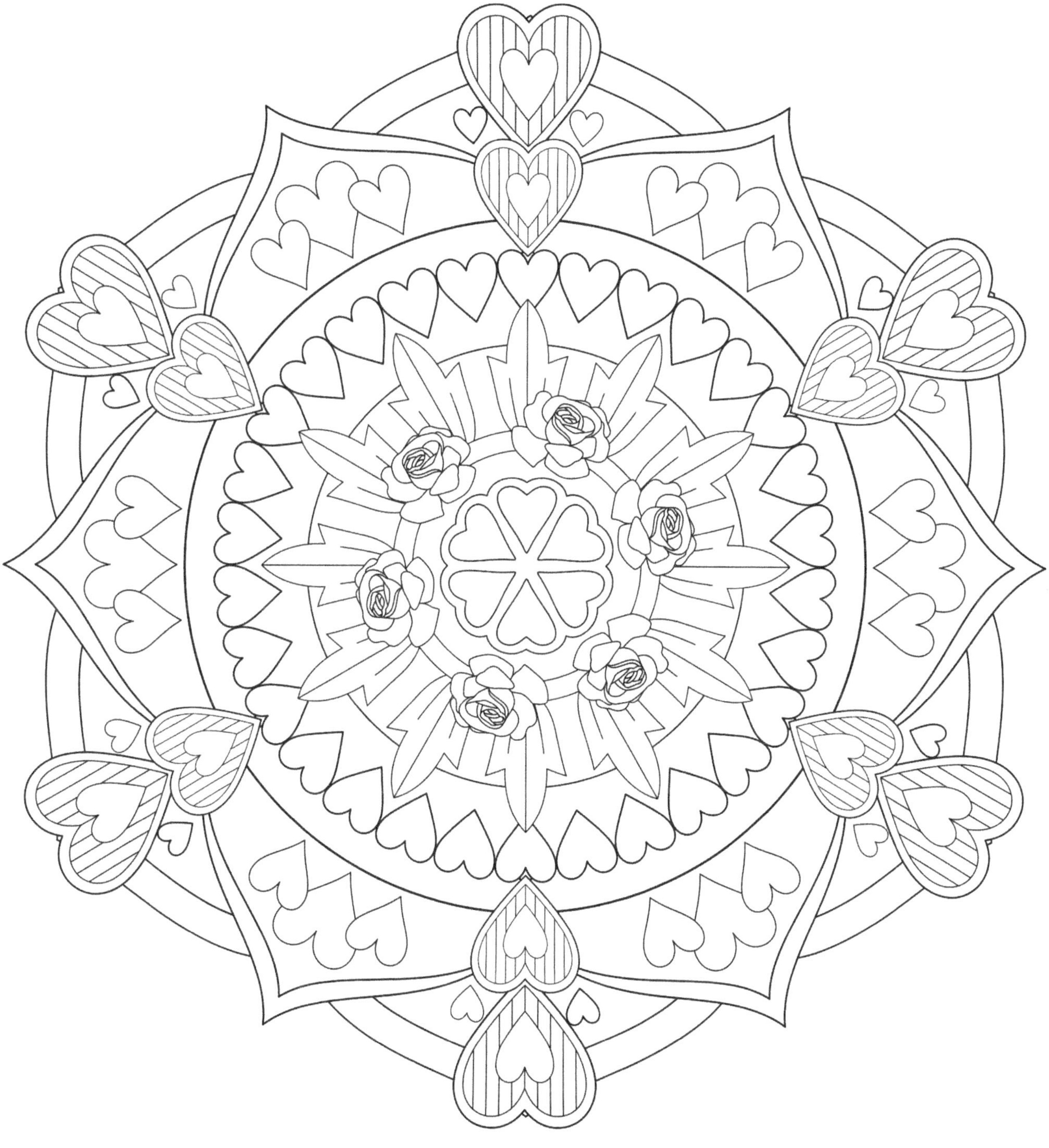

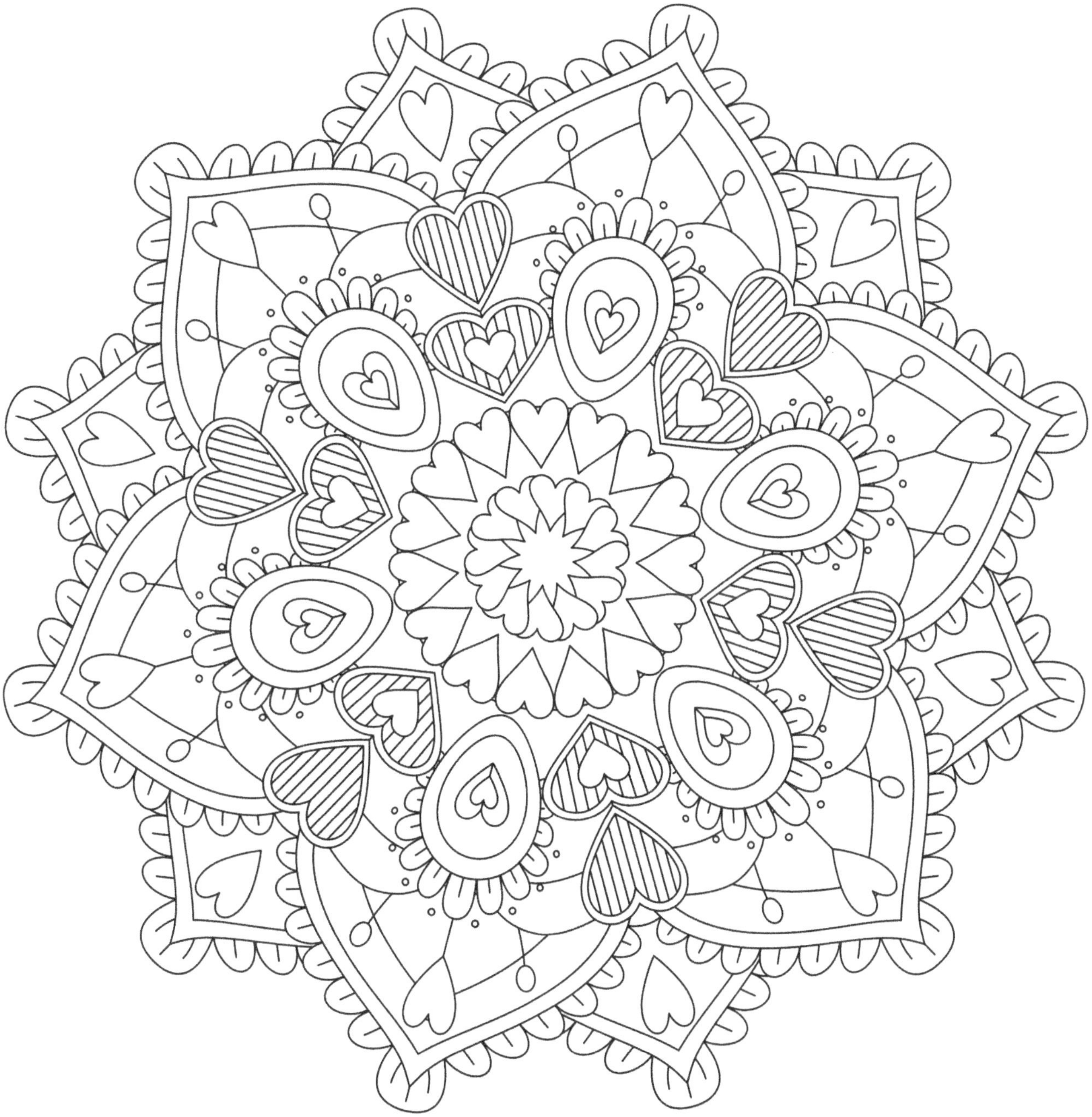

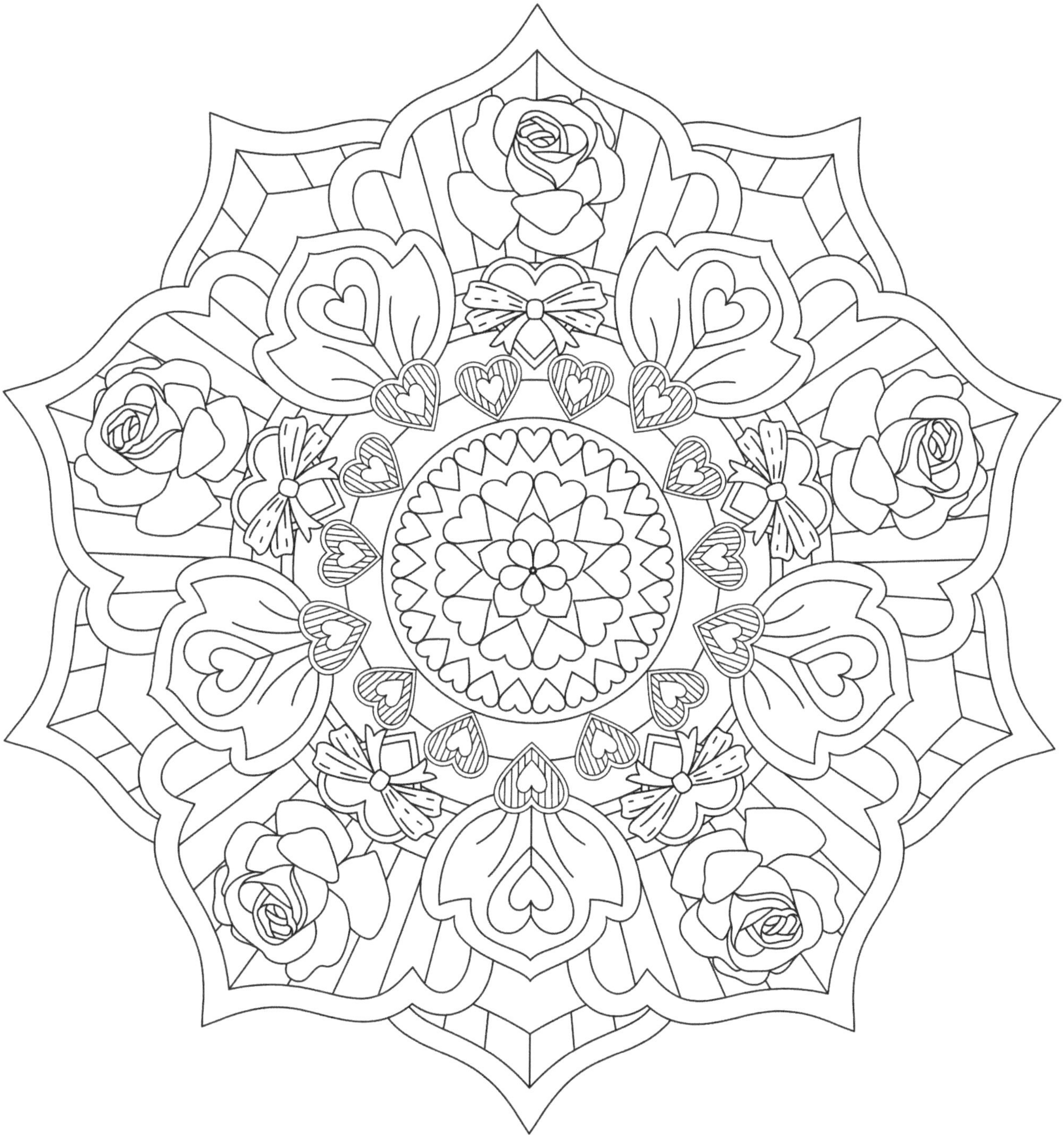

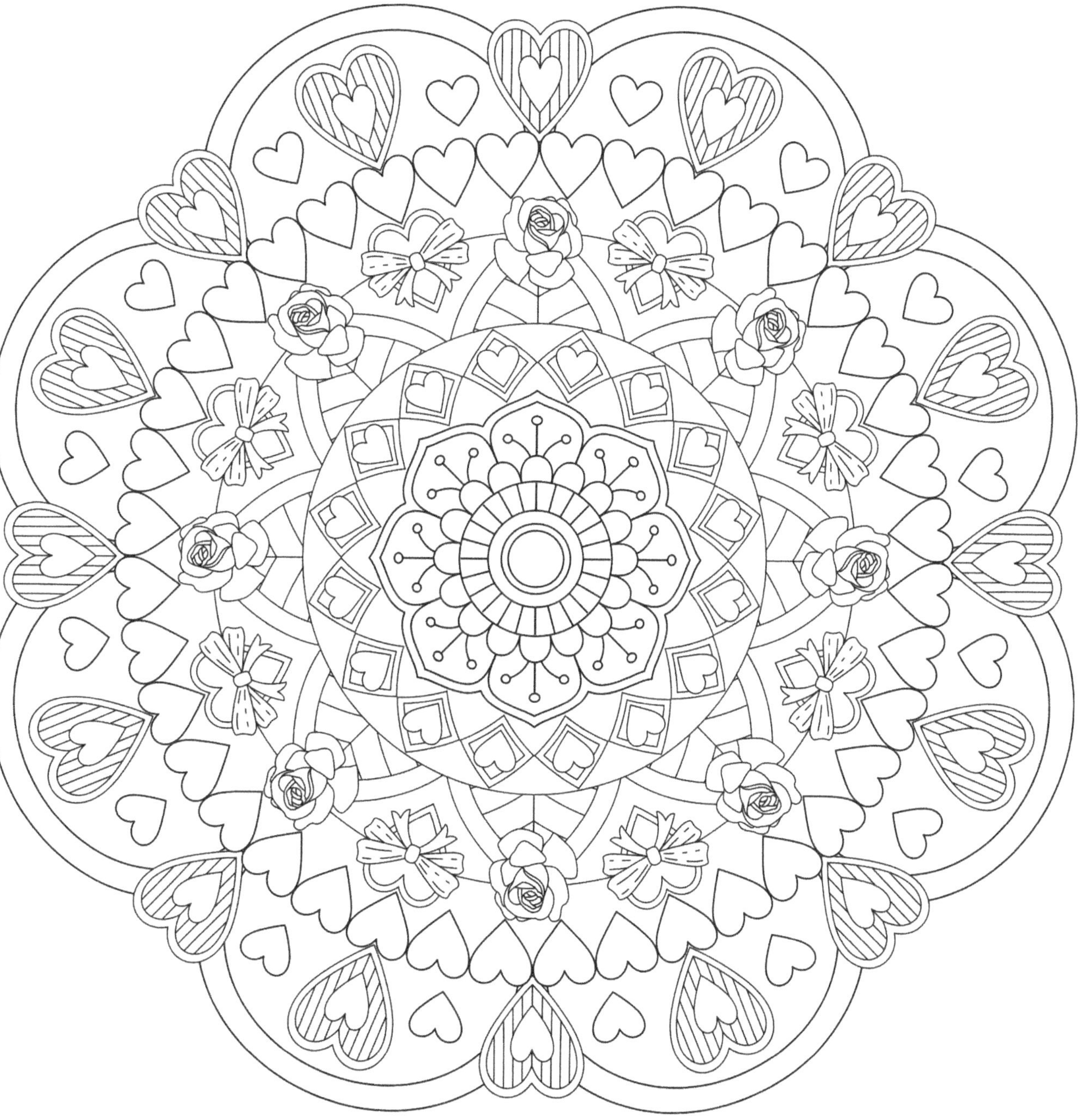

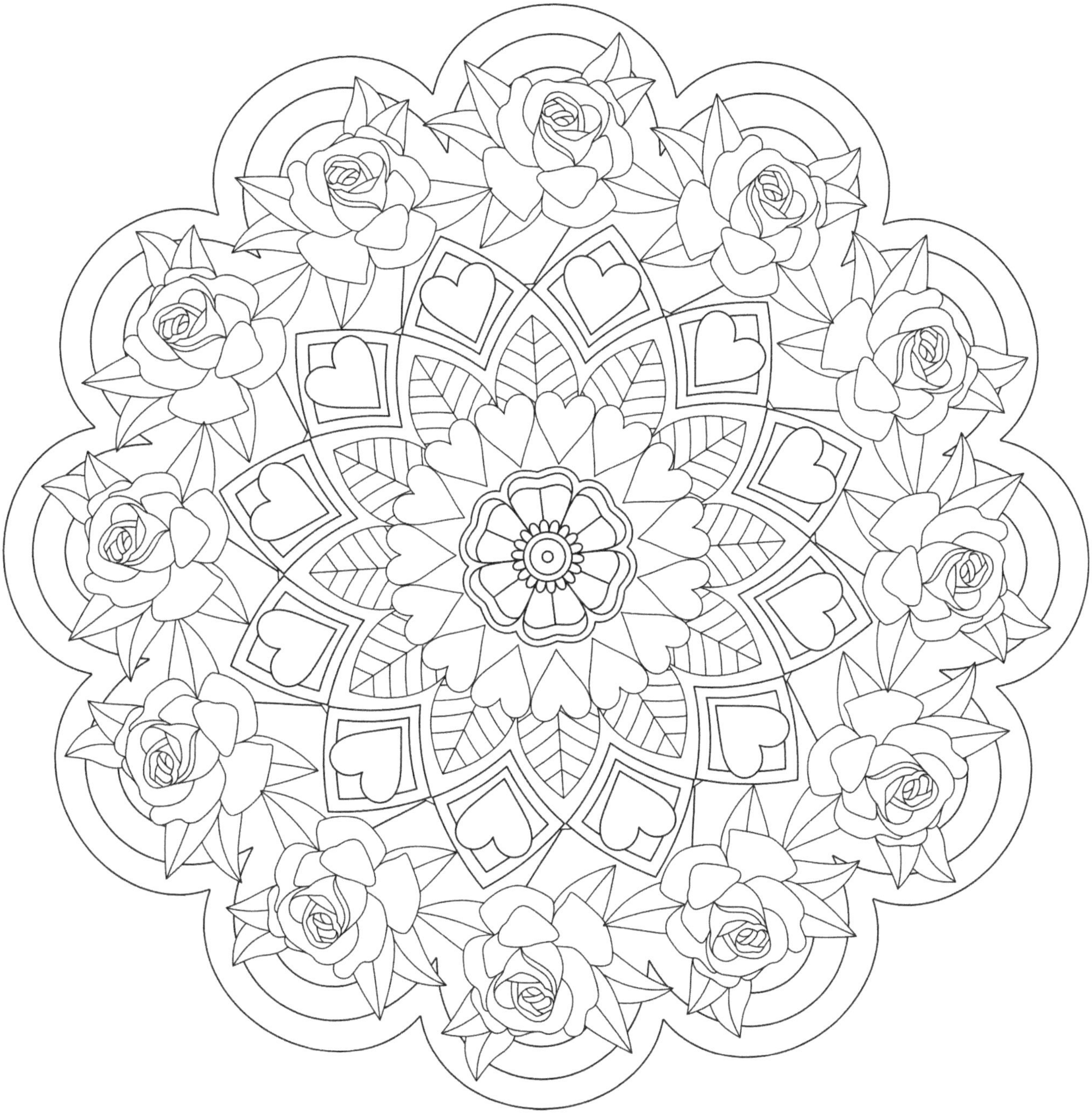

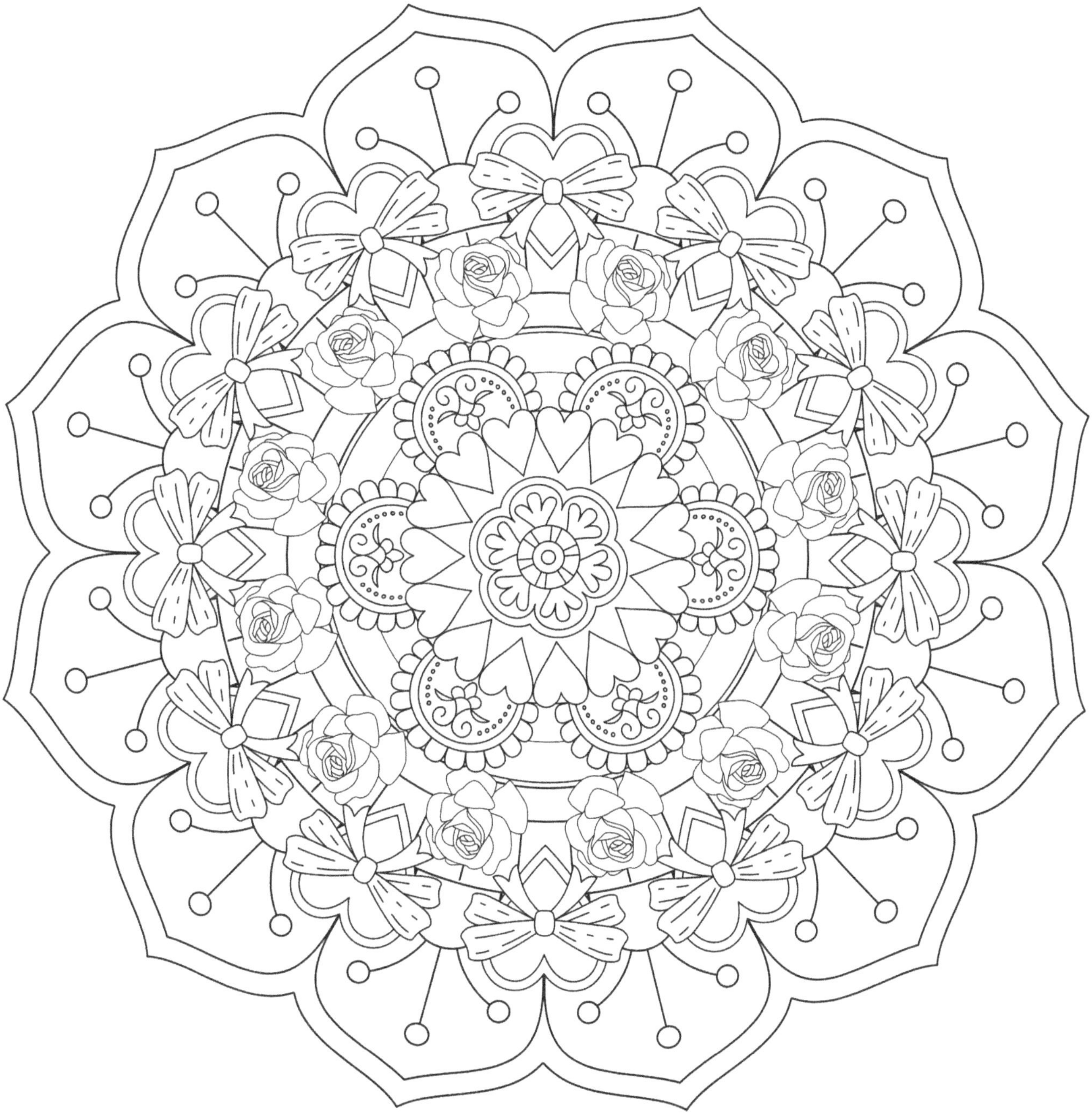

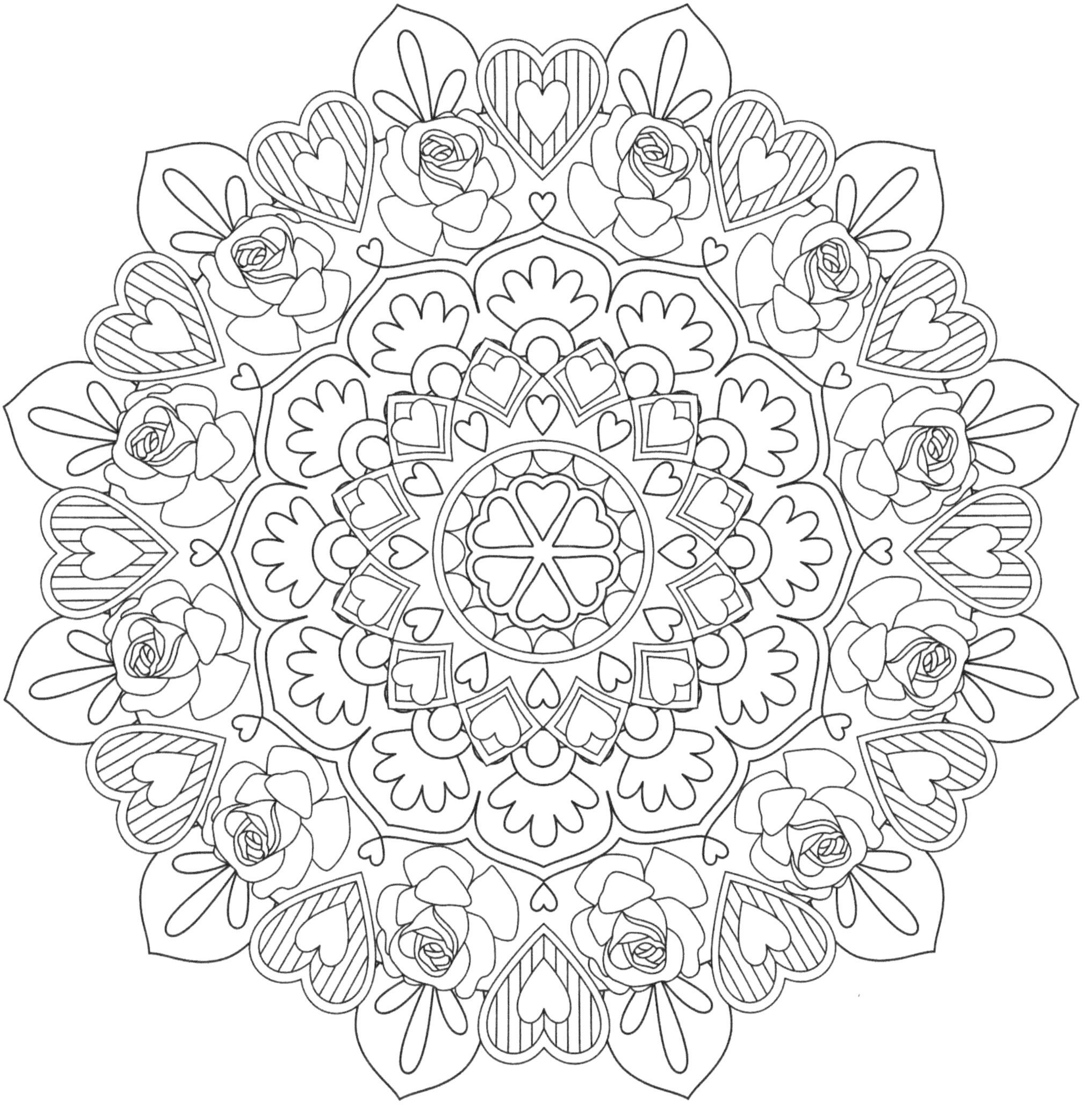

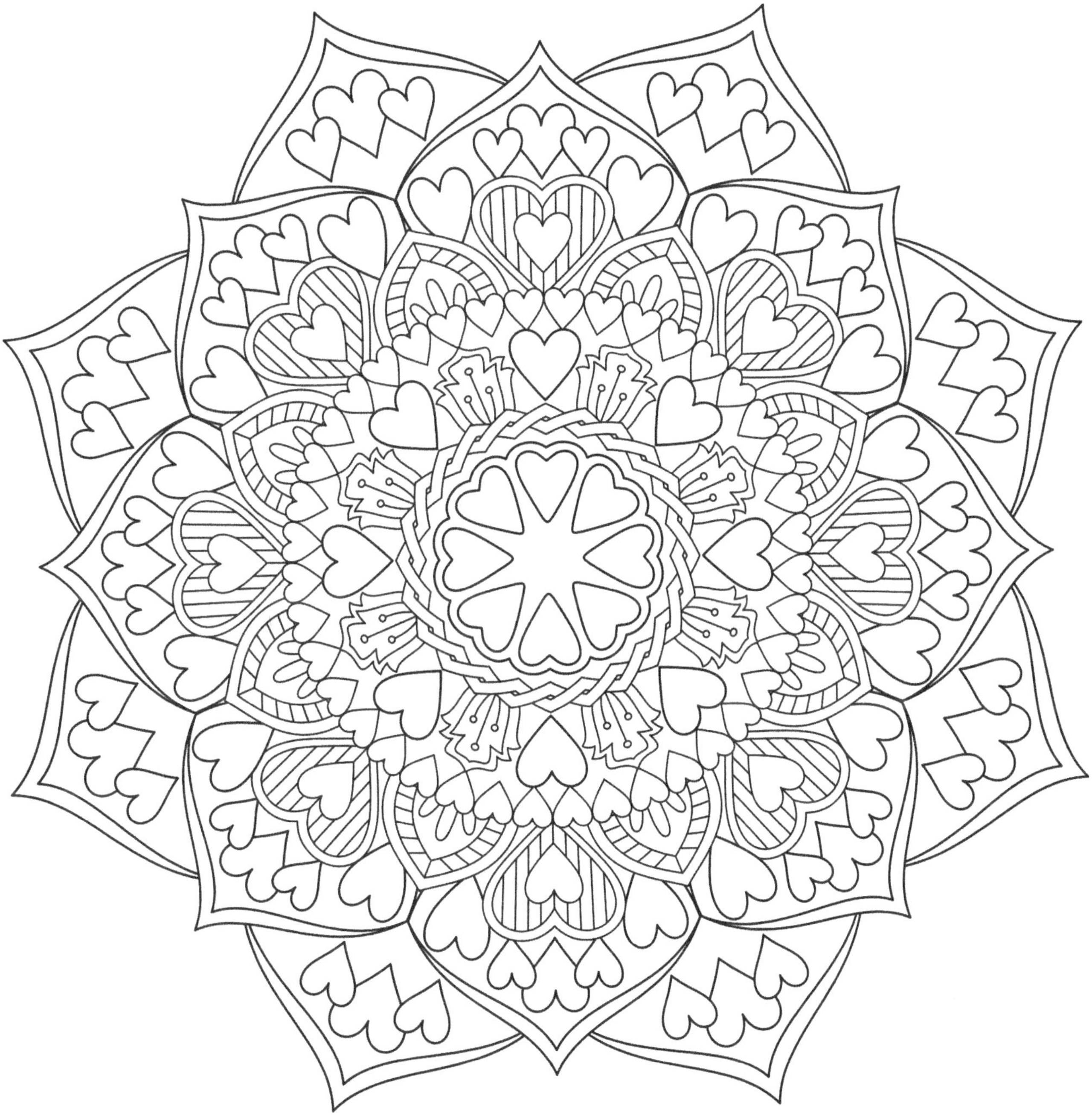

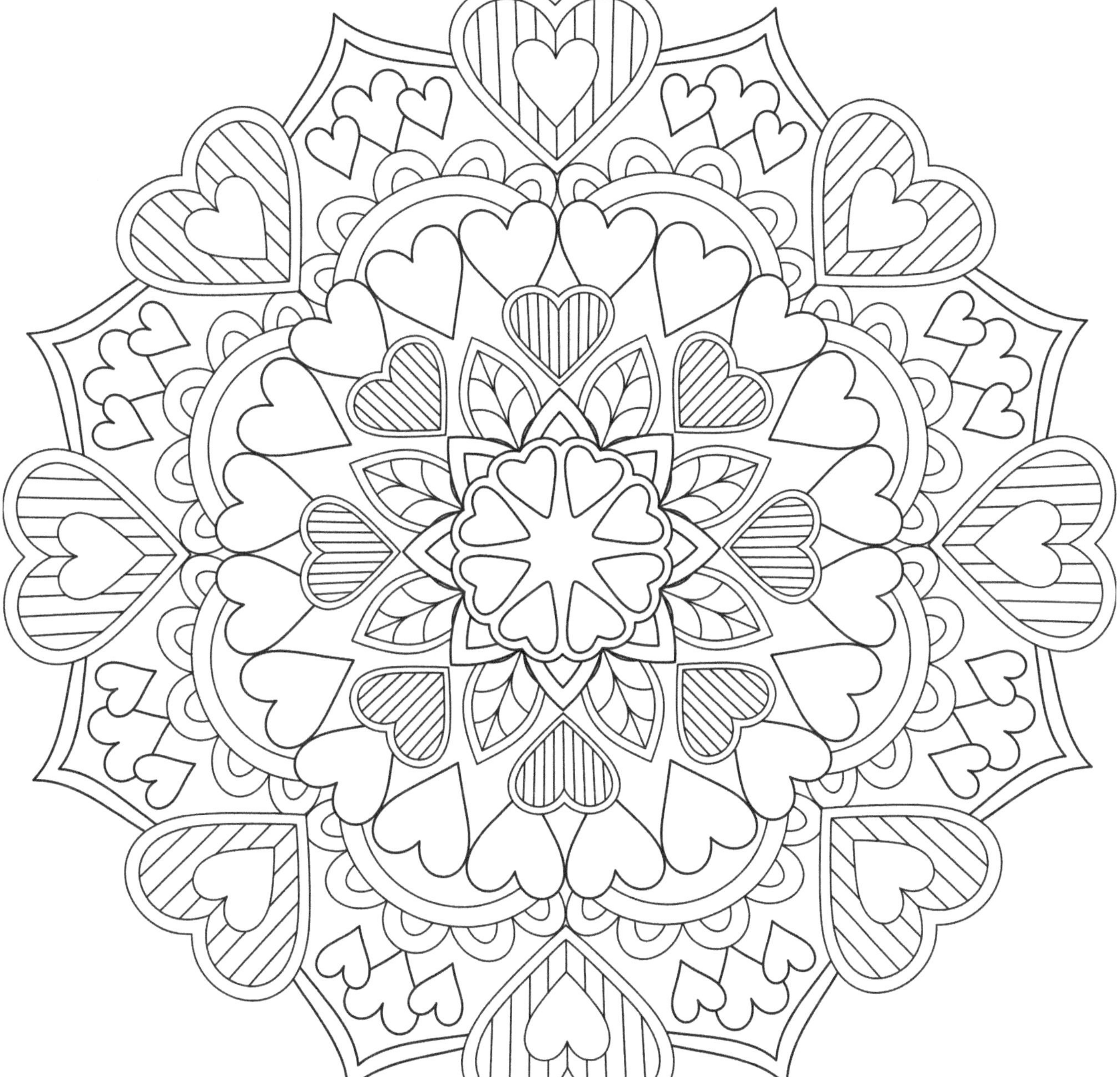

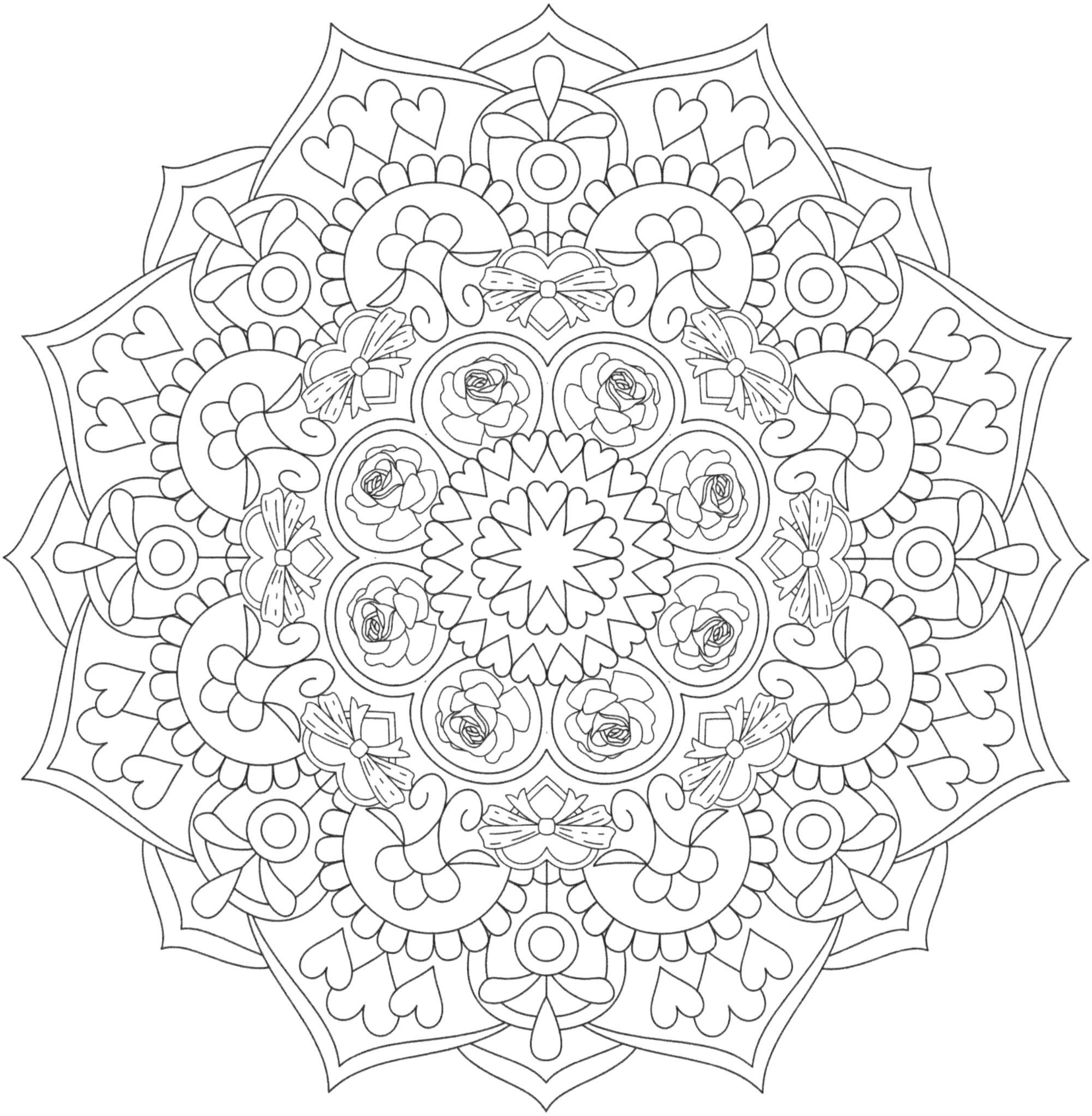

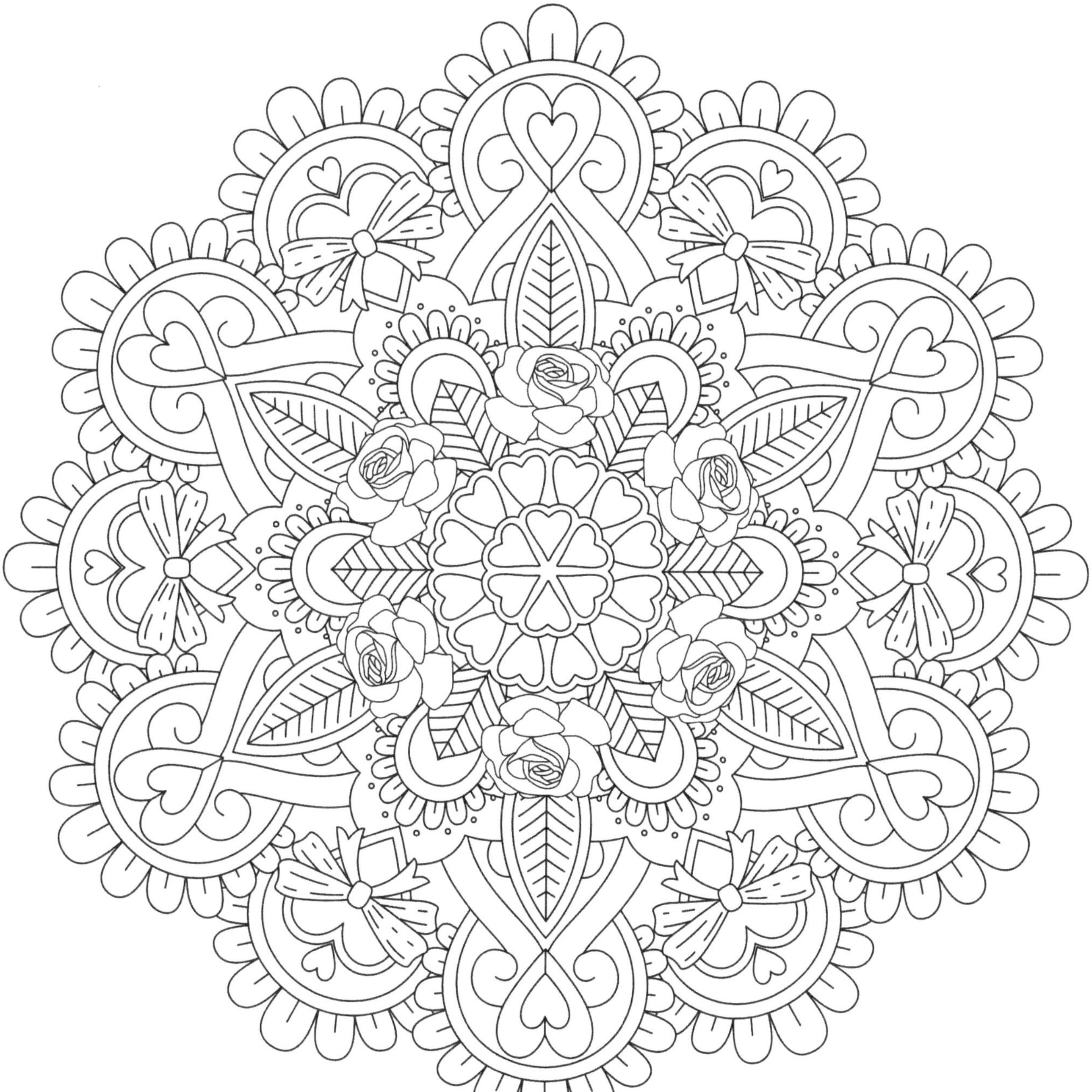